A-B-C Critter Cafe

Deana Carmack

Graph Publishing, LLC
110 N. Seaman St.
Eastland, Texas 76448

Title: A-B-C Critter Café
Subtitle: Revised Edition
© Deana Carmack, 2020

All rights reserved. No part of this publication may be reproduced or transmitted by any means-- manual, electronic, mechanical, photocopying, or recording without prior written permission from the author, except by a reviewer, who may quote brief passages in a review.

Title: A-B-C Critter Café
Author: Deana Carmack
Illustrations: Deana Carmack
Illustration media: watercolor, acrylics, colored pencil

Back Cover Photograph: Aaldeidah, Pixabay

Summary: A series of twenty-six alphabetized animals including jingles involving their alliterative eating preferences…portrayed in humorous and colorful formats…useful for teaching the alphabet, animal recognition, rhyme and rhythm schemes, poetic meter and alliteration.

Library of Congress Cataloguing in Publication Data education, literature, general-juvenile literature

Classification Categories: General Education; Early Childhood Education, Elementary Education

Printed in the United States of America
ISBN: 978-1-7345142-9-2

Mr. Marcellus, the mighty mouse, minces mangoes in his house.
He munches them down to the seed inside...
then throws the pit away.

M m

O o

Oscar, the playful little otter,
eats oats and oranges in the water,
and olives, okra, and Oreos, too,
with an ornery brother named
Oliveroo.

P p

Pete, the perky pelican,
picks peanuts,
as well he can.
He packs them into his
enormous pouch
To save for a rainy day.

R r

Reba, the racing roadrunner, tries
round, red radishes before she flies.
and raisins and raspberries,
and all fruits red
before running away
to her roadrunner bed.

S s

Sidney, the soft and silky sable
savors soup without a table...
or napkins or plates,
or even a tray...
he sips with his tongue

then skitters away.

Ulani, the unique unicorn,
unpacks her lunch with a single horn.
An umbrella keeps the sun at bay
as she daintily nibbles away.

U u

Willy, the wily baleen whale,
wants wiggly seaweed in his pail.
In all that wet water,
         he's sure to find
enough to eat his fill.

W w

"X" is for the X-opation,
a critter from imagination.
His tail is long;
his wings are short;
crunching "X's"
is his sport.

X x

Look over yonder at the Asian yak.
Yertle likes yummy yams for his snack.
He's young and slow with a ruffle on his back.
Wouldn't you like to ride on a yak?

Y y

Jackrabbit and kangaroo have their own brand of hopping;
Roadrunner and mouse skitter on without stopping.
The horse and the unicorn trot up a hurry;
The quail and the vulture fly in with a flurry.
Elephant and yak come plodding along,
While baboon and newt arrive, singing a song.
The fox and the crocodile are sporting a smile,
But gorilla and llama hang back for a while.
The pelican and toucan are starting to move;
X-opation and dinosaur have found their own groove.
Iguana and sable sassily sashay,

As they all make their way to the

Ranjithsiji, Pixabay

www.ingramcontent.com/pod-product-compliance
Lightning Source LLC
Chambersburg PA
CBHW042032100526
44587CB00029B/4391